J 338.761 Lon
London, Martha,
Minecraft /
$25.00   on1122857009

T5-ACZ-560

WITHDRAWN

OUR FAVORITE BRANDS

MINECRAFT

By Martha London

WORLD BOOK

Bigfoot Books

The Quest for Discovery Never Ends

This edition is co-published by agreement between Kaleidoscope and World Book, Inc.

Kaleidoscope Publishing, Inc.
6012 Blue Circle Drive
Minnetonka, MN 55343 U.S.A.

World Book, Inc.
180 North LaSalle St., Suite 900
Chicago IL 60601 U.S.A.

All rights reserved. No part of this book may be reproduced in any form without written permission from the publishers.

Kaleidoscope ISBNs
978-1-64519-016-5 (library bound)
978-1-64494-181-2 (paperback)
978-1-64519-116-2 (ebook)

World Book ISBN
978-0-7166-4316-6 (library bound)

Library of Congress Control Number
2019904237

Text copyright ©2020 by Kaleidoscope Publishing, Inc. All-Star Sports, Bigfoot Books, and associated logos are trademarks and/or registered trademarks of Kaleidoscope Publishing, Inc.

Printed in the United States of America.

FIND ME IF YOU CAN!

Bigfoot lurks within one of the images in this book. It's up to you to find him!

TABLE OF
CONTENTS

Chapter 1: Block by Block **4**

Chapter 2: A New Way to Play **10**

Chapter 3: A World as Big as Your Imagination **16**

Chapter 4: Always Expanding **22**

Beyond the Book *28*

Research Ninja *29*

Further Resources *30*

Glossary *31*

Index *32*

Photo Credits *32*

About the Author *32*

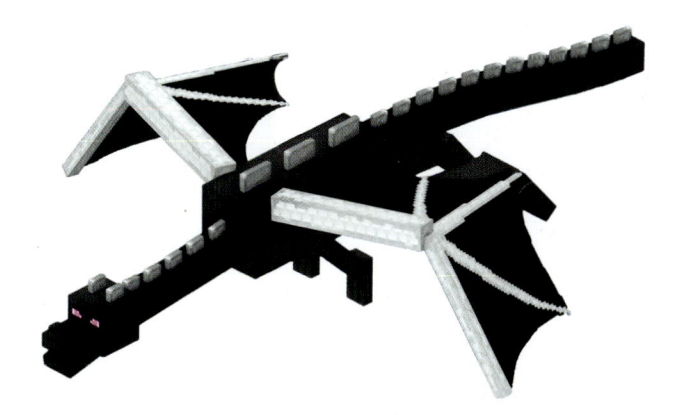

CHAPTER 1

Playing Minecraft *is a favorite activity among many young people.*

FUN FACT

Very rarely, *Minecraft* appears misspelled as "Minceraft" on the introductory screen.

Block by Block

Jordan sits on her bed. She opens up her laptop. She just finished eating with her parents. It's time to play *Minecraft*. Jordan watches her screen change. She enters a new world.

Everything is made up of 3-D blocks. Inside those blocks are materials. Jordan can **mine** the materials. She smashes the blocks with her axe. Jordan needs to make a new house. She starts cutting trees down. She is playing in survival mode. Her character is getting hungry. She needs to find something to eat.

Jordan also needs to watch out for enemies. Groups of monsters could attack. Jordan loses her materials if her character dies. When she **respawns**, she has to gather them again.

Jordan doesn't have to be in survival mode. There's also creative mode. But in creative mode, everything is already given to her. She doesn't have to work for anything.

Students in France built a Minecraft replica of their city.

Jordan thinks survival mode is more fun. She has to solve problems. She feels proud when she builds something. It means she found all the materials she needed. It feels more like a typical video game.

Sometimes she plays in creative mode to try new things. It's fun to see what she can make. Some players have made **replicas** of famous buildings and places.

Jordan loves *Minecraft*. She even plays it in school. Her teacher used it in a lesson about buildings in history. Someone in her class made a building from Greece. Jordan made one of the pyramids in Egypt. It was fun to learn using *Minecraft*.

Minecraft *lets people play and work together.*

Jordan also likes that she can play with other people. Sometimes she plays with her classmates. Together they can build amazing things. Jordan likes working with her friends. It's easy to solve problems with their help.

9

CHAPTER 2

A New Way to Play

Markus Persson was bored. He loved making computer games. He even worked for the biggest game company in Sweden. But the games weren't his. He wanted to design his own. The company wouldn't let him do that. He didn't have enough spare time to make games after work. Persson decided to quit his job. It was time to make his own game.

There was just one problem. He didn't know what he wanted to make. Persson went online looking for inspiration. He was in a group with other game **developers**. People in the group called him "Notch." They shared new games they were making. The group tested each other's games. "Notch" got a lot of ideas from this group. They encouraged him.

FUN FACT
Minecraft was originally called *Cave Game*.

Markus Persson worked at a video game company, but he wanted to have more freedom to design his own game.

Persson spent many hours **coding**. He wanted to make a whole world. The game started off underground. There were brown and gray cubes. His **avatar** used an axe to break up the blocks. Then his avatar could use the pieces to make new objects. He could make bridges and buildings. He was excited.

INFINIMINER

Other video games inspired *Minecraft*. One of those was *Infiniminer*. The game looks a lot like *Minecraft*. Everything is made of 3-D blocks. The blocks hold resources. *Minecraft* and *Infiniminer* have one major difference. *Infiniminer* is competitive. *Minecraft* is more about the fun of building.

Minecraft *features blocks and cubes, which players mine and then use to build new objects.*

The group of developers tried out the game. Everyone loved it. They helped fix problems in the game. But Persson was running out of money. He needed money to keep working on the game full-time. He picked a number: thirteen. He would sell his game for thirteen dollars. That sounded like a fair price. He hoped people bought his game.

They did. And people kept buying it. Soon, more than one thousand people were playing *Minecraft*. People started making whole cities. They built rocket ships. Boats sailed on the water. Players made underground forts. The possibilities were endless. *Minecraft* had become a hit.

Minecraft allows players to build complex, detailed structures.

HOW PEOPLE PLAY MINECRAFT
IN NORTH AMERICA

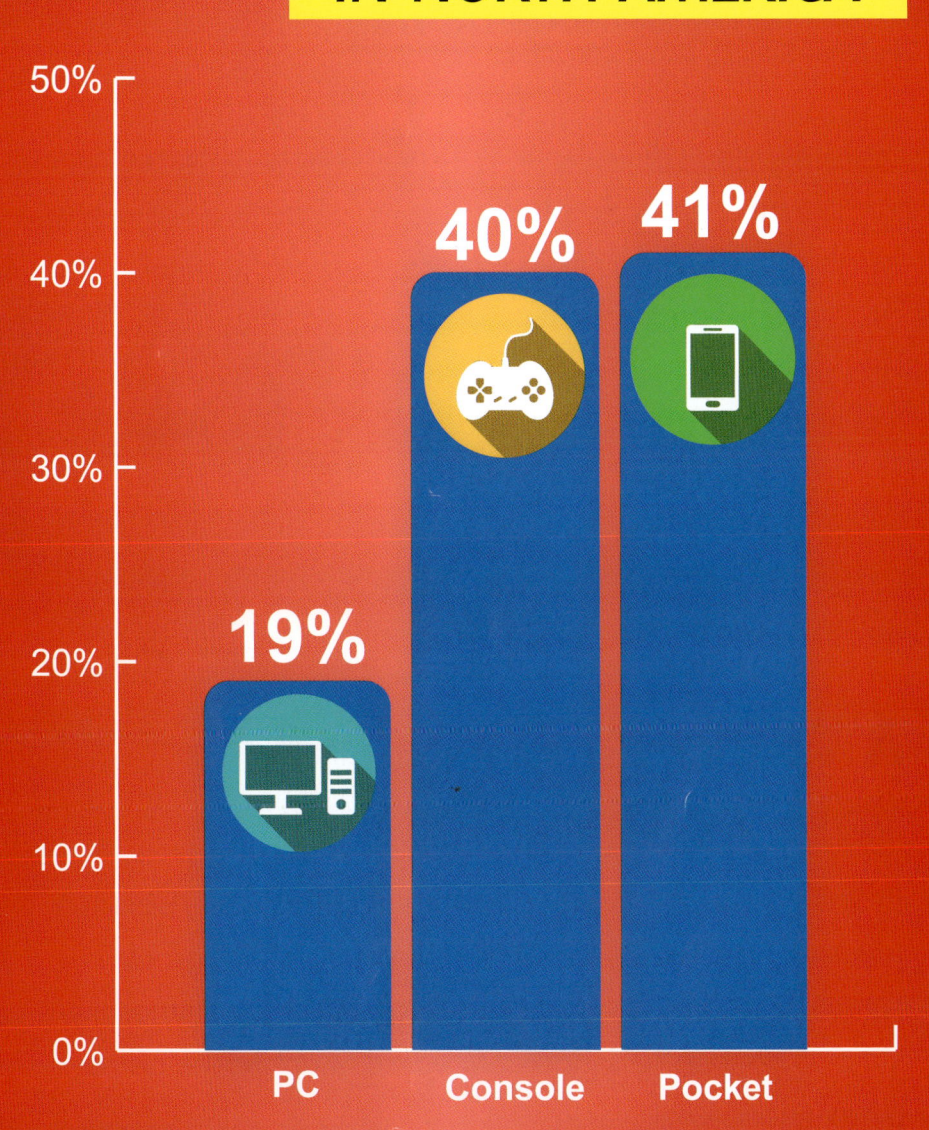

Platform	Percentage
PC	19%
Console	40%
Pocket	41%

CHAPTER 3

People can play Minecraft *on phones, video game consoles such as Xbox and PlayStation, and computers.*

A World as Big as Your Imagination

In 2014, Microsoft bought *Minecraft*. One player, Ben, has been playing *Minecraft* for years. He's a huge fan. He was nervous when Microsoft took over the game. What if Microsoft changed *Minecraft*? Luckily, the game didn't change.

FUN FACT
Telltale Games released an interactive show called *Minecraft: Story Mode* on Netflix in 2018.

Ben's family doesn't have a computer or an Xbox. But he has a smartphone. He plays *Minecraft* on his phone. Ben likes that he doesn't need an expensive computer. There are a lot of games he can only play at his friends' houses. He can play *Minecraft* wherever he wants.

Even better, Ben can connect with his friends. Some play on computers. Others play on game consoles. It doesn't matter what kind of technology they have. The *Minecraft* world is the same. They can still play together.

He can even play with his friends at school. His teacher made a math lesson using *Minecraft*. Ben thought that was weird. He thought *Minecraft* was for building and making.

But his teacher showed the class something cool. She explained how to find out how big their creations would be in real life. Ben liked that lesson. He found out that one of his buildings was actually pretty big.

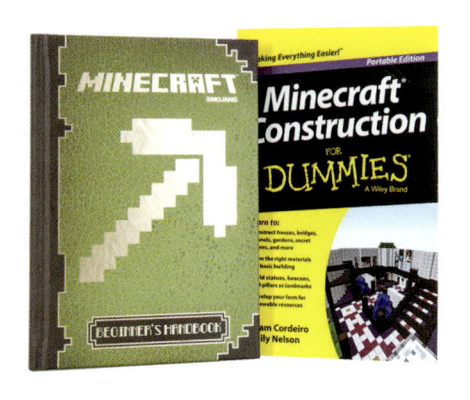

Some teachers have used Minecraft *in their classrooms to teach lessons on math, history, and technology.*

MINECRAFT BOOKS

Minecraft is expanding beyond the digital world. People have written game guides. They help players learn new skills. There are books that tell stories about the *Minecraft* universe. They make up adventures for characters. Some of the books are best sellers.

LEGO started releasing Minecraft sets a few years after the game first became available.

Ben was excited when *Minecraft* and LEGO started working together. He bought a few of the sets. It's fun to build the *Minecraft* world in real life. He likes the Crafting Box set most. The pieces can be used in different ways. Some of the other sets only have one way to build. But the Crafting Box has many options.

CHAPTER 4

Always Expanding

Minecraft's first two years were a big success. Ten million people downloaded the game. By the end of 2018, more than 154 million copies of *Minecraft* had been sold. The game is still growing. That means *Minecraft*'s world is growing. Players all over the world are making new things.

Li lives in China. She plays *Minecraft* often. *Minecraft* is a special game. Players like Li can make changes to the game. Li has a powerful computer. She makes **mods** for *Minecraft*.

Minecraft *continues to grow and attract new players.*

Minecraft *players with enough coding experience can build mods for the game. They can share these mods with other players.*

Some mods are small. But some are huge. Players recreate TV shows. Others make new **scenarios**. Li creates new environments. She loves making underwater worlds. Li loves this part of *Minecraft*. The game is never boring. There are always new things to build or explore.

The best part is that Li can share her mods. Players around the world can use them. They don't need special technology. Even a player on a smartphone can use Li's mods. Li likes that *Minecraft* is for everyone.

Some players attend Minecraft events to meet and play the game with other fans.

24

If Li wants to play *Minecraft* with others, she can. She loves working with other players. But sometimes she wants to build by herself. Li plays music in the background. Sometimes the music inspires her to make something. Li's apartment is small. But she has fish. She loves watching them swim. Their fins float as they move. Li's fish tanks inspire her mods.

Li is part of a community. She feels connected to other players making mods. Li doesn't feel like she's waiting for new adventures. She knows someone is already working on the next one. Sometimes, she's the one creating it. Tomorrow, *Minecraft* will be just a little bit different. Li can't wait to see what it holds.

FUN FACT

The language of *Minecraft*'s Endermen characters is just English in reverse or lowered in pitch.

MINECRAFT
TIMELINE

2009
Markus "Notch" Persson begins creating *Minecraft*.

2011
Minecraft: Pocket Edition is released.

2006 2007 2008 2009 2010 2011 2012

2010
An **alpha** version of the game is released in June.

2012
Minecraft is available on Xbox 360.

LEGO releases its first *Minecraft* set.

26

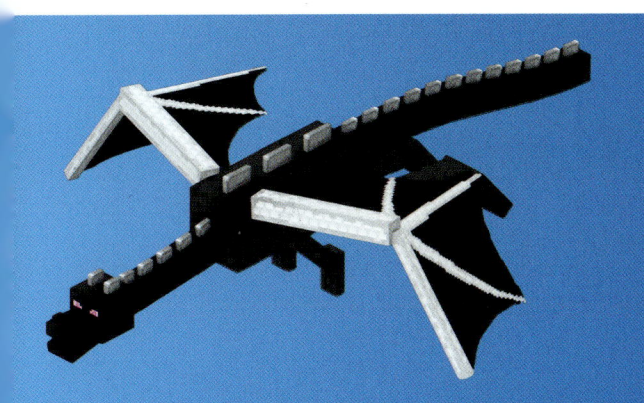

2018
More than 154 million copies of *Minecraft* have been sold.

2014
Microsoft buys *Minecraft* for $2.5 billion.

2017
The "Better Together Update" allows players on different platforms to play together.

| 2013 | 2014 | 2015 | 2016 | 2017 | 2018 | 2019 |

2014
Minecraft: Realms becomes available worldwide.

2016
Minecraft: Education Edition is released.

2019
Minecraft: Dungeons is released.

27

BEYOND
THE BOOK

After reading the book, it's time to think about what you learned. Try the following exercises to jumpstart your ideas.

THINK

DIFFERENT SOURCES. What kinds of sources might have more information about *Minecraft*? How could each of these different types of sources be useful in its own way?

CREATE

SHARPEN YOUR RESEARCH SKILLS. Think about how teachers use *Minecraft* in the classroom. Where could you go in the library, or who could you talk to, to find more information about using *Minecraft* in schools? Create a research plan by writing a paragraph that details the next steps for research.

SHARE

SUM IT UP. Write a paragraph that summarizes the most important points from the book. Make sure you write it in your own words. Don't just copy the text. Then share your paragraph with a classmate. Does your classmate have any feedback on the summary or additional questions about *Minecraft*?

GROW

DRAWING CONNECTIONS. Create a diagram that shows and explains the connection between *Minecraft* and computer coding. How does learning about computer coding help you better understand *Minecraft*?

RESEARCH NINJA

Visit **www.ninjaresearcher.com/0165** to learn how to take your research skills and book report writing to the next level!

RESEARCH

DIGITAL LITERACY TOOLS

SEARCH LIKE A PRO
Learn about how to use search engines to find useful websites.

FACT OR FAKE?
Discover how you can tell a trusted website from an untrustworthy resource.

TEXT DETECTIVE
Explore how to zero in on the information you need most.

SHOW YOUR WORK
Research responsibly—learn how to cite sources.

WRITE

GET TO THE POINT
Learn how to express your main ideas.

PLAN OF ATTACK
Learn prewriting exercises and create an outline.

DOWNLOADABLE REPORT FORMS

Further Resources

BOOKS

Bedell, J. M. *So, You Want to Be a Coder?: The Ultimate Guide to a Career in Programming, Video Game Creation, Robotics, and More!* Aladdin / Beyond Words, 2016.

Future Publishing. *Cool Builds in Minecraft!* Scholastic, 2018.

Zeiger, Jennifer. *The Making of Minecraft.* Cherry Lake Publishing, 2017.

WEBSITES

Factsurfer.com gives you a safe, fun way to find more information.

1. Go to www.factsurfer.com.
2. Enter "Minecraft" into the search box and click 🔍.
3. Select your book cover to see a list of related websites.

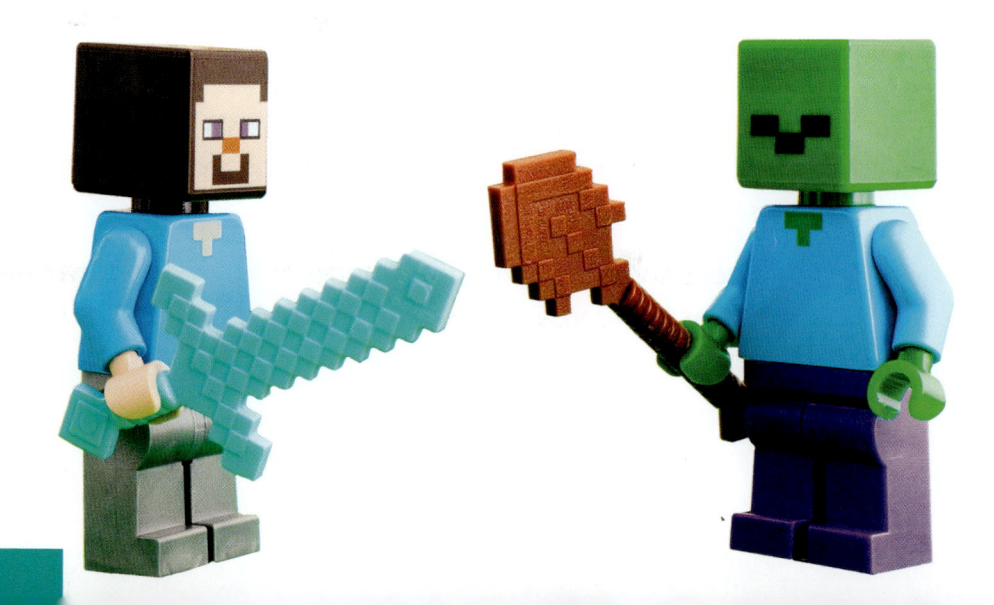

Glossary

alpha: An alpha version of a game is the first version. The alpha edition of *Minecraft* was released in 2009.

avatar: An avatar is the character someone plays in a game. Ben wanted his *Minecraft* avatar to look like him.

coding: Someone is coding when they create a computer program or game using a computer language. The students were coding a program that made a tree on the computer screen.

developers: People who work on making games or computer programs are called developers. The developers in Persson's group helped him to make the best game he could.

mine: To mine means to take materials out of something, usually dirt and rocks. Players in *Minecraft* need to mine tools and materials out of the blocks.

mods: Mods are modifications, or changes, made to something, such as software. *Minecraft* allows players from all over the world to build mods for the game.

replicas: Replicas are objects built to look like other objects. The players made replicas of their houses.

respawns: A character or avatar in a video game respawns, or comes back to life, after it dies. In *Minecraft,* the avatar respawns where it last slept.

scenarios: Scenarios are different adventures or tasks for a player to try. The first time Jordan played *Minecraft*, she wanted to try easier scenarios.

Index

books, 20

consoles, 15, 17–18, 26–27

creative mode, 6–7

development, 12, 14

devices, 5, 15, 17–18, 22–23

Dungeons, 27

Education Edition, 27

Infiniminer, 12

LEGO, 21, 26

Microsoft, 16, 27

mods, 22–23, 25

Persson, Markus "Notch", 10, 12, 14, 26

Pocket Edition, 15, 26

Realms, 27

replicas, 7–8

sales, 14, 22, 27

scenarios, 23

schools, 8, 18–19

Story Mode, 17

survival mode, 5–7

timeline, 26–27

PHOTO CREDITS

The images in this book are reproduced through the courtesy of: Iuskiv/Shutterstock Images, front cover (background); Pabkov/Shutterstock Images, front cover (person); pio3/Shutterstock Images, front cover (wolf); Alainara/Shutterstock Images, pp. 3, 27 (top); Bloomicon/Shutterstock Images, pp. 4–5; Alexandre Marchi/PhotoPQR/L'est republicain/MAXPPP/Newscom, pp. 6–7; wavebreakmedia/Shutterstock Images, pp. 8–9; REDPIXEL.PL/Shutterstock Images, pp. 10–11; Chesnot/Getty Images Entertainment/Getty Images, pp. 12–13; Georg Wendt/picture-alliance/dpa/AP Images, p. 14; Red Line Editorial, p. 15 (chart); tulpahn/Shutterstock Images, p. 15 (electronics icons); Tinxi/Shutterstock Images, pp. 16–17; Michael Penn/The Juneau Empire/AP Images, pp. 18–19; urbanbuzz/Shutterstock Images, pp. 19, 27 (bottom right); TanyaLovus/Shutterstock Images, pp. 20–21; CTR Photos/Shutterstock Images, pp. 21, 26 (bottom); bibiphoto/Shutterstock Images, p. 22; Dragon Images/Shutterstock Images, p. 23; Paul Hennessy/Polaris/Newscom, pp. 24–25; Pavel Kapysh/Shutterstock Images, p. 26 (top); Ekaterina_Minaeva/Shutterstock Images, pp. 27 (bottom left), 30.

ABOUT THE AUTHOR

Martha London lives and writes in Saint Paul, Minnesota. She likes to read and go for hikes in the woods.

Harris County Public Library, Houston, TX